Falling For You in the Midst of Autumn

Always Agust

BookLeaf
Publishing

Presentation by *BookLeaf Publishing*

Web: www.bookleafpub.com

E-mail: info@bookleafpub.com

ISBN: 978-93-95784-50-4

First edition 2022

DEDICATION

Dedicated to the love of my life

Like Honey and Tea

Falling for you, as the leaves fall from trees.
I fell for you, in the cool autumn breeze.

In your eyes, is where I find peace.
Your eyes are warm, like honey and tea.

Falling and falling, ever so deep.
From the cold, they're my only relief.

My Favorite Sweater

Your love feels like the sweater,
That I've always worn.
I know as we enter winter,
I'll always be warm.

No matter the weather,
That we may encounter,
This love is enough,
From now, till forever.

Dreaming

Drinking coffee,
Drinking tea,
Sitting on the rocking porch swing.

Together, I hold you and you hold me.
Warm in your arms, watching falling leaves.

Gently and softly, we fall fast asleep.
Dreaming of us, forever and always.

Falling With The Leaves

When I met your eyes,
My heart skipped a beat.

In the autumn breeze,

The leaves called out,
"Please fall with me."

Making Room For You

5

People say spring is made of new beginnings,
But autumn is the one that made room for them.

This autumn is making room in my heart,
I'll spend all of my autumns with you.

From here, on.

Autumn Outside Of A Post Office

Outside the post office,
Leaves on the ground.
Sitting on the park bench,
Scanning the crowd.

And there I see you,
Smiling so bright,
Coming across the bridge,
My gaze softens at the sight.

September

Your presence is like the wind,
that gives me chills.

That's what if feels like,
Every time our hands meet.

My body starts to shiver as I smile,
And my heart beats wildly.

Coffee Shops

Stopping at a coffee shop,
Walking through the door.
Lattes and baked goods,
As we watched the rain pour.

It was warm inside,
Compared to the rainy autumn weather.
My heart would beat for you,

"I'm so happy we're together."

October

This year in October,
I want to be yours.
I decided the costume,
As soon as you walked through that door.

I hope you'll be mine,
This Halloween.
Matching costumes,
You and me.

Blankets

1st of September,
Windows open.
Curled up in blankets,
My heart so outspoken.

The cool wind enters,
This room so full.
Filled with our love,
The warmest thing I know.

Leaves fall softly.
As the wind helps them fly.
Traveling for miles,
So far, so high.

On adventures,
like us,
In falling in love.

My Autumn Clouds

Your love is like the autumn clouds,
That summer always lacks.
Protecting me from the heat,
That I never l liked.

You protect me from the stress,
That this world has to offer.
Like the autumn clouds protect me,
From the hot summer weather.

Setting Sun

12

The sunset is orange,
Like the colors falling from the sky,
On this chilly autumn night.

Staring at your eyes,
Brown like the colors,
that float so high.

Pumpkins

Our love story is in the making,
Like the pumpkins,
we are carving.

They sit outside the doors,
Of every house we walk in.

Seasons

Autumn reminds us that some things must end.

Loneliness ended with
Summer,

So our love could begin in
Autumn,

And happiness will grow in
Spring.

Warmest Love

15

You're like a warm cup off coffee,
In the morning
Of this beautiful season.

I Picked You

I don't need a perfect one,
Just one that I can love.
Picking out a pumpkin,
That I'll be able to carve.

I don't need someone perfect,
I just need you.
And we'll shape our love,
The way it works for us.

Mine To Hold

From coffee dates,
To mornings under the covers.
Whenever we are together,
All I see are the prettiest colors.

Holding your heart,
Here in my arms.
I promise I'll keep it safe,
And we'll never have to part.

God Is The a Best Artist

You took me to the museum,
Full of beautiful work.
Holding your hand warms my heart,
Walking through these halls.

"You're my favorite piece of art."

Thunderstorms

I like autumn thunderstorms,
So I can say I'm scared.
And you pull me in closer,
To relieve all of my fears.

Cozy Drinks

Autumn is like coffee,
With colorful shades of brown.
But bitter like the cold,
Until you came around.

You added sugar to the coffee,
I drink in autumn.
Our love speaks volumes,
And will continue to blossom.

My Favorite Season

Falling for you,
In the midst of this season.
The best one, I think.

Do I need a reason?

Now it will always be my favorite,
Because you came along.
You stole my heart,
In the middle of fall.

And our love will grow,
Like the pretty spring flowers.
Because autumn brought us together,
So we could start over with each other.